Finding Your Purpose in Christ

Matthew Robert Payne

This book is copyrighted by Matthew Robert Payne. Copyright © 2016. All rights reserved.

No part of this publication may be reproduced, stored in a retrieval system or transmitted in any way by any means, electronic, mechanical, photocopy, recording or otherwise, without the prior permission of the author except as provided by USA copyright law.

To sow into Matthew's writing ministry, to request a personal prophecy or life coaching or to contact him, please visit http://personal-prophecy-today.com.

This book was edited by Lisa Thompson. You can email her at writebylisa@gmail.com or visit her website at www.writebylisa.com.

Cover designed by akira007 at fiverr.com.

Unless otherwise indicated, all Scripture taken from the New King James Version. Copyright © 1982 by Thomas Nelson, Inc. Used by permission. All rights reserved.

Scripture quotations are taken from the Holy Bible, New Living Translation, copyright ©1996, 2004, 2007, 2013, 2015 by Tyndale House Foundation. Used by permission of Tyndale House Publishers, Inc., Carol Stream, Illinois 60188. All rights reserved.

The opinions expressed by the author are not necessarily those of Revival Waves of Glory Books & Publishing.

Published by Revival Waves of Glory Books & Publishing PO Box 596| Litchfield, Illinois 62056 USA
www.revivalwavesofgloryministries.com.

Revival Waves of Glory Books & Publishing is committed to excellence in the publishing industry. Book design Copyright © 2016 by Revival Waves of Glory Books & Publishing. All rights reserved.

Paperback: 978-1-68411-156-5

Hardcover: 978-1-68411-157-2

Dedication

I dedicate this book to the Holy Spirit who guides me with many things that I do. Thank you so much for being in my life and giving me your counsel.

Acknowledgements

I want to thank Jesus for being my friend and the Holy Spirit for guiding me and Father God for overseeing them both. I want to thank my mother for being my friend and someone I can talk to. I want to thank my friends, Praying Medic and Michael Van Vlymen, for being great Christian friends in my life.

I want to thank my cover designer Akira007 on Fiverr.com and my editor, Lisa Thompson, for her careful work with my books. I want to thank Bill Vincent of Revival Waves of Glory Books and Publishing for publishing this book for me.

I want to thank the readers for whom I write. I hope you are touched by these simple words that were written for you. I hope this is not the last book you read of mine.

Table of Contents

Dedication   iii

Acknowledgements iv

Table of Contents v

A Note from My Editor vii

Introduction   ix

CHAPTER 1: 1

    The Meaning Of Life...1

    What Drives You?...5

    What Is Important to You? 6

    What Is Important to God? 7

    How to Reconcile Both..9

CHAPTER 2: 12

    The Shifting Sands, The Unfruitful Vine......12

    50 Commands of Jesus 15

    Becoming Separate from the World...............21

    How to Divorce the World 24

CHAPTER 3: 27

    Life Founded On The Rock..........................27

    How to Love God and Your Neighbor............31

CHAPTER 4: 34

    Finding Your Purpose 34
    What Do You Feel You're Meant to Do? 35
    What Does God Say? 37
    What Do Prophets Say? 38
    Could You Arrange to Do that Job? 39

CHAPTER 5: 41

    Living Your Purpose 41
    You Are Loved Already 42
    Moving into Your Desired Work 44
    Finding Fulfilling Part-Time Occupations ... 46

CHAPTER 6: 49

    Storing Of Rewards In Heaven 49
    How Do We Store up Rewards in Heaven? ... 51
    What Does Reward Have to Do with Purpose?
    55
    I'd love to hear from you 57

How to Sponsor a Book Project 59

    Other Books by Matthew Robert Payne 61

About the Author 63

A Note from My Editor

Matthew asked me to write a quick note about this book. He is a treasure to work with, and I was so honored that he asked me to share.

I have had the privilege of editing seven of Matthew's books to date. We spend time on Skype, going through the edits word by word, in hopes that we can provide the readers with a book that clearly communicates Matthew's passion for the subject at hand. He feels a great compassion for you, the reader, and if he had his way, he would sit down and talk with you over a cup of coffee about each of these subjects.

Since he can't do that, he does the next best thing — shares his heart through his books. We live in such an amazing time when technology allows people like Matthew to self-publish and connect with readers globally.

Honestly, this is one of my favorite books that I have edited so far for Matthew. He handles this topic — much needed in the Body — with such practicality. You will **not** find a bunch of spiritual mumbo jumbo here that leaves you scratching your head, wondering what to do next! Instead, you will find content rich with step-by-step actions that you can take today to move you toward finding your purpose in Christ.

If you are looking for an editor who will work closely with you on your manuscript, I would love to speak with you.

My website is: www.writebylisa.com, or you can email me at writebylisa@gmail.com.

Blessings and happy reading to you!

Introduction

With the confirmation of my personality type as an ENFJ, according to the Meyers-Briggs temperament analysis, I was born to be a gifted communicator. My temperament leans toward championing people and encouraging them. I found this out at age 30.

Nineteen years later, I am communicating via a blog and by writing books and running groups on Facebook. I often motivate people in my writing, and I also encourage people through my prophetic gift.

We all have a purpose, and we all need to find it. If we don't find our purpose and live it out, our life might seem meaningless and wasted. The sad thing is that many Christians live this way all their life.

In order for us to find our purpose, we might need to do some digging and research and take some risks. I write to you today to compel you to seek out your purpose and take the risks you need to take to pursue it.

As a person who has found his purpose and is living it, I felt qualified to write this short book for you.

Dive in!

CHAPTER 1:

The Meaning Of Life

The Meaning of Life

People often ponder, "What is the actual meaning of life?" Many people live a life as a Christian in this world where they wander from place to place, always wondering about the meaning of life. They ask themselves what their purpose is.

Many philosophers and people who expound on eternal truths wonder about this question. I first had this question answered in a helpful way by a saint that I met.

I have a strong relationship with Jesus Christ. Just like Jesus met Moses and Elijah on the

Mount of Transfiguration, I also have the ability to meet saints from heaven.

One time, one of the saints from heaven spoke to me. He told me that the meaning of life is to find out what your purpose is in life and to do it with such excellence that you bring glory to God.

In order to find the meaning of life, you first have to find your purpose for living. When you find your purpose for living, you need to walk out that purpose in such an extraordinary way that people cannot help but look to God in amazement. In this way, God is glorified.

Some people really have a huge impact on this world. Consider people like Steve Jobs in this generation — a man who started a software company in the garage of his mother's house.

Steve and his friend designed the Apple computer. They originally sold it to an electronic store in a kit on how to build a computer. From there, they went on to form Apple, one of the finest and most successful corporations in the world.

Apple is renowned for the high quality of their products, dominating the world market. Steve was just a man who found his niche. He was just a man who found out why he was here. He did it in such an extraordinary way.

Many people are proud of him and happy with the impact that he made. He not only had an extraordinary effect in the world of computers, but he also founded a company called Pixar Animation. Pixar, along with a partnership with Disney, has produced more than 20 best-selling films.

In fact, all of the films that Pixar has released have been an outstanding success, which is quite rare in Hollywood. Hollywood regularly seems to have films that are flops and that don't do well at the box office. Pixar, Steve Jobs' company, has reversed that trend and been successful with every film that has been made by them.

With this in mind, Steve Jobs found his purpose as an engineer and in creating, designing, and by being the CEO of a company. With his technical ability, his attention to detail and his personality of perfection, he built and managed the company that dominated in the world. He did it in such a great way that his life brought glory to God as his Creator.

We can also look at the life of Mark Zuckerberg. Mark once was a student who got an idea for a computer program to connect people at the university that he attended. He built this computer program, put together a list of people and started what he called "The Facebook." Later on, they dropped the "The" and called the program Facebook.

Once again, he was a man with a history in programming. He went against all odds and developed a company that is now a world leader. Facebook helps everyone who is interested communicate on the internet via social media in a more satisfactory and beneficial way.

The people that I know around the world through Facebook are amazing. It extends your reach and expands the influence that you have in the world. Facebook is an extraordinary company that is always updating its program. It's always improving, always becoming something better.

Once again, an engineer started the original program and went on to oversee and become the CEO of a company that has dominated in the world. First, we need to find our purpose in the world. Then, we need to grow and fulfill that purpose in such a way that it brings glory to God.

According to many people, Steve Jobs and Mark Zuckerberg were not Christians. Even so, they have made God look good. When people really succeed in the world, it shows the capacity that people have for achieving huge personal success. Whether we know it or not, it increases our faith and our love for God the Creator.

God is the mastermind behind every person; he receives the glory when we accomplish significant feats in this world.

What Drives You?

First of all, if you are going to find your purpose in life, you have to realize what drives you. My personality is very interested in educating Christians. My passion is to find answers for the Christian world. Then, I present those answers in books, articles and blog posts for Christians to read.

I have a passionate desire to see the Kingdom of God advance in the world. I want Christians to be all that they can be. I want to see Christians fulfilling everything that they were created to do.

That is what drives me. What drives you? What is it that really makes your heart burn? What makes your engine start? What model is the engine in the car of your soul? What really turns you on?

You have to find this answer within yourself. You have to look within yourself and see what it is that excites you. What is it that you want to do? How do you want to impact the world? What is important to you?

What Is Important to You?

For me, like I've said, it's important for people to be educated and motivated to become all that they can be — to reach their full potential. Just the idea of writing this book and presenting it comes from the idea that I want to educate people. I want to encourage them to be everything that they want to be.

The idea for this book came tonight. Here I am today, recording the content that will be typed up and made into a manuscript. It's important to me that Christians are not lukewarm. I strive to help Christians be effective in this world. I want to ignite passion in others and motive them to be good soldiers in the fight to bring Christ and his way and his Kingdom to earth.

What is important to you? What do you want to see changed? What affect do you want to have in this world? What ways do you want to impact the world and bring change? Or are you happy with aimlessly wandering through life and leaving the world as it is?

Are you happy with what is happening at the moment? Are you a person who admires others or who admires a certain lifestyle? Do you admire a certain occupation and want to be part of that occupation?

What is it that is important to you? This is one of the key fundamental questions that you have to ask yourself. You have to know the answer to this question if you are going to find your purpose.

I am a person with the ability to prophesy and to hear from God. I can operate as a prophet. I can also communicate through writing a book, editing it and readying it for publication and the market. I write interesting books so that I can be a success as a writer. I can speak, and I will preach in the future as well.

This gives you an idea of some things that are important to me, things that I am good at. I also have a vision for my future and of how I will succeed. You have to work out what is important to you and then pursue that in order to find your purpose.

What Is Important to God?

You might never have considered this important question before. You might not have ever taken the time out of your busy day and life to ponder this topic. What is important to God? We find an interaction in the Scriptures that points us to what is important to God.

Luke 10:25-28 says, "And behold, a certain lawyer stood up and tested him saying, 'Teacher, what shall we do to inherit eternal life?' He said to them, 'What is written in the law? What is your reading of it?' So he answered and said, 'You shall love the Lord your God with all your heart, with all your soul, with all your strength, and with all your mind and your neighbor as yourself.' And he said to him, you have answered rightly. 'Do this and you will live.' "

We see that Jesus sums up what is important for eternal life in this passage. He says that a person is to love God with all their heart, soul and mind and to love their neighbor as themselves.

Here, Jesus provides a summary of all of his commandments. Love your God with your entire being and love your neighbor. God prioritizes these actions.

Some people might fail in that regard. They might fail to love God with all their heart, mind and soul or fail to love their neighbor as themselves. This is called "sin" or "falling short."

When we really look at life — at what a righteous life is — the difference between living a life of mediocrity and living righteous and holy is our ability to love God and our neighbor with a love that is complete and perfect.

The answer to what God thinks is important is the job that helps you to love God with all your heart, mind and soul and to love your neighbor. How can you best love God with all your mind, heart and soul? How can you best love your neighbor? We will come back and answer this question later in the book.

How to Reconcile Both

As such, we need to work out what is important to us and work out what is important to God and reconcile both of them.

Personally, I have a heart for God's people. I have a heart that loves the people of God and that loves the Christians in this world. I want to better educate them and help them become more successful Christians.

I love God so much that I am able to feel and hear his heart on certain issues. I can then take that love for God and use it as motivation to write and go through the process of paying for and publishing books that will better educate the people of God.

First of all, I love God. I have compassion for others because of my love for him. This manifests further when I write for my fellow Christians. I love them by producing material that will benefit them so that they can build their lives on something solid.

My purpose in life is to educate Christians and to empower them to live a more prosperous and successful life. Everything that I do with my life is aligned with educating and better informing Christians.

You might be a doctor or a lawyer. If so, you need to find a way to better serve God and others in your work, no matter your profession.

Of course, you will obviously help those who are sick, provide diagnoses and cure their ills and diseases as part of your profession. You will pursue justice, not matter which side of the case you represent. However, you can also make a more immediate impact.

You can pray with your patients. You can say to them, "God Bless you. I'll pray for you." You can extend a strong Christian influence in your medical or legal practice. You can better affect the people that you serve.

It might be hard sometimes to be a criminal lawyer or work in the legal field and keep your sanity and your integrity with God.

I have watched many legal shows. The practice of law seems to be a very slippery slope. But you can stand out and make a difference. You can make an impact as a lawyer.

You can work with integrity and refuse to take on cases that compromise your faith. You can stand out as an example in the cases that you do take. You can make a difference to the people that you interact with. Everywhere we go as a Christian, we can make an impact and a difference.

We need to look at our jobs and our purpose and at what is important to us. We need to reconcile how we will accomplish that. We need to find out how we can better love God and better love our neighbor in the process of fulfilling our dreams.

When you find out what is important to you and determine how to reconcile that with what is important to God, then you will have started on the journey toward your destination.

CHAPTER 2:

The Shifting Sands, The Unfruitful Vine

Shifting Sands and Unfruitful Vine

Matthew 7:24-27 says, "Therefore whoever hears these sayings of mine and does them, I will liken him to a wise man who built his house on the rock: And the rain descended, the floods came, and the winds blew and beat on that house; and it did not fall, for it was founded on the rock. But everyone who hears these sayings of mine and does not do them, will be like a foolish man who built his house on the sand: and the rain descended, the floods came, and the winds blew and beat on the house; and it fell. And great was its fall."

These shifting sands do not provide a firm foundation for our lives. Jesus came to earth to show us a way — not only to live a righteous life and die as a sinless sacrifice for the forgiveness of sins but to be an example of how we can live by his life and his preaching. He shared with us the ways to life abundant and how we can live the best possible life. It is up to us to live a life that is obedient to what he said.

Matthew 13:22 talks about the unfruitful vine. " Now he who received seed among the thorns is he who hears the word, and the cares of this world and the deceitfulness of riches choke the word, and he becomes unfruitful."

We see a contrast between the shifting sands and the unfruitful vine. Building your life on shifting sands means that you fail to obey the commandments of Jesus Christ. The shifting sands represent the fact that we are building our life on something that isn't stable, something that isn't solid. Jesus clearly said that the person who hears what he is teaching and applies it in their life is the person who's built their house upon the rock.

Then, he went on to say that those people that heard the same thing but that didn't apply what was taught in their life are the people that are building their life on shifting sand. They are people that are building their life on something that isn't stable.

When persecution or trouble comes, their house and everything that is important to them will be crushed and defeated. Our world at the moment is experiencing much grief, sadness and tribulation. However, you can still disobey the commands of Jesus Christ yet have a relatively successful life.

A time is coming in this world when things will become a lot darker, and persecution will come. Pressures will make life a lot harder to live.

In those times, the people that are living their life in obedience to what Jesus taught will have more of a solid foundation for their life. Jesus wants us to not only read what he taught, but he wants us to actually obey his words as well.

Again, to emphasize, this verse, Matthew 13:22 says, "Now he who received seed among the thorns is he who hears the word, and the cares of this world and the deceitfulness of riches choke the word, and he becomes unfruitful."

Jesus spoke specific commands and gave teachings on the way that you should live your life. But people let the cares of this world, the ways of this world and the deceitfulness of riches actually choke out the Word of God. They make the Scripture to no effect.

They are like thorns that choke a plant and stop the plant from producing fruit. Many Christians are living this sort of life. Many Christians have one foot in the world and one foot in the Kingdom of God.

A high percentage of Christians in this world simply do not know how to live a life that is holy and set apart for God. This theme is common throughout my books. I like to teach people that they need to be separate from the world. We'll talk about that more very soon.

50 Commands of Jesus

I asked my mother to make a summary of Jesus' commands in the Gospels. She went through the Gospels and recorded every time that Jesus told us to do something or when Jesus said not to do something. We called these the "commands of Jesus" after what he said in John 14:21.

This verse says, "He who has My commandments and keeps them, it is he who loves Me. And he who loves Me will be loved by My Father, and I will love him and manifest Myself to him."

Jesus is clearly saying that the people who have his commandments and who keep them are the people that love him. These words are for those in the Christian church. Our Bibles have the commandments of Jesus, which are scattered throughout the Gospels.

I am going to include a copy of the 50 commandments of Jesus Christ with Scripture references so that you will have them. You can look up the verses and see that Jesus actually did say them.

1. *Don't call Jesus Lord when you don't obey him. Luke 6:46; Matthew 7:21.*

2. *Build on the rock of obedience to Jesus, or you will fall. Matthew 7:24-27; Luke 6:47-49.*

3. *Worship God alone. Matthew 4:10b; Luke 4:8.*

4. *Follow Jesus. Matthew 4:19, 11:28-30; Mark 1:17; John 1:43, 12:26, 10:27, 21:22b.*

5. *Be salt and light to this world. Matthew 5:13-16; Mark 9:50; Luke 11:33, 14:34; John 3:21.*

6. *Don't call your brother a fool. Matthew 5:22, 12:36.*

7. *Practice instant reconciliation. Matthew 5:24-25.*

8. *Do not look with lust at another, or you commit adultery in your heart. Matthew 5:27-28.*

9. *Do not divorce and marry another; this is adultery. Matthew 5:32, 19:9; Mark 10:11-12.*

10. Don't swear an oath. Matthew 5:33-37.

11. Do more than expected; go the second mile. Matthew 5:38-41.

12. Give to those that ask. Matthew 5:42; Luke 6:30, 38.

13. Love, bless and pray for your enemies. Matthew 5:43-48; Luke 6:27-29.

14. Quietly do good for God's praise alone. Matthew 6:1-4.

15. When you pray, fast or give, do it secretly. Matthew 6:5-6.

16. Don't use vain repetitions when praying. Matthew 6:7-8; Mark 12:40.

17. Pray to God the Father. Matthew 6:9, John 16:23-24.

18. Don't be anxious. Matthew 6:25-32; Luke 12:22-30; John 14:1, 16:33.

19. Store up your riches in heaven, not on earth. Matthew 6:19-21, 33; Luke 12:21, 31-34; John 12:25.

20. Judge not that you may not be judged. Matthew 7:1-5; Luke 6:37, 41-42; John 7:24.

21. Keep asking, seeking and knocking. Matthew 6:9-11, 7:7-11; Luke 11:9-13.

22. Treat others as you like to be treated. Matthew 7:12; Luke 6:31.

23. Don't waste time on argumentative people. Matthew 7:6.

24. Forgive others. Matthew 6:12, 14-15, 18:21; Mark 11:25-26; Luke 11:9-13.

25. Let the dead bury their dead. Matthew 8:22; Luke 9:6a.

26. Don't fear people, fear God. Matthew 10:28, 16:23; Luke 12:4-5.

27. Confess Christ before men. Matthew 10:32-33; Mark 5:19, 8:38; Luke 9:26, 12:8-9.

28. Take up your cross. Matthew 10:38-39; 16:24-26; Mark 8:34-37; Luke 9:23-26, 14:26-33.

29. Beware of hypocrisy and greed. Matthew 15:6-9, 23:28; Luke 6:41-42, 12:1b, 20:46-47.

30. Privately rebuke a brother and if he repents, forgive him. Matthew 18:15; Luke 17:3-4.

31. Pay your taxes and give to God what is his. Matthew 22:21; Mark 12:17; Luke 20:25, 21:4.

32. Love God and others. Matthew 22:37-40; Mark 12:30-31; Luke 10:27; John 15:12, 13:34-35.

33. Keep alert and watch for the second coming. Matthew 24:44, 46, 50-51; Mark 14:62; Luke 12:35-40, 21:27-28.

34. Honor God with all that you have been given. Matthew 25:14-31; Luke 18:18.

35. Minister to others as you would to Jesus himself. Matthew 25:34-46.

36. Preach the Gospel and teach obedience. Matthew 28:20; Mark 16:15; Luke 9:60b; John 21:15b, 16b, 17b.

37. Repent of your sins. Mark 1:15; Luke 13:3,5, 15:7,10, 18-24.

38. *Believe in Jesus. Mark 16:16; Luke 9:35; John 6:29, 12:36, 14:6, 20:29.*

39. *Have childlike faith. Mark 10:15; Luke 18:17; Matthew 9:29.*

40. *Don't sell things in God's house. Mark 11:15-17; John 2:16.*

41. *Rejoice when you are persecuted. Luke 6:22-23.*

42. *Don't be distracted from hearing God's Word. Luke 10:38-42.*

43. *Act with compassion and not prejudice towards others. Luke 10:30-37.*

44. *Invite the poor to eat with you. Luke 14:13-14.*

45. *Humble yourself and take the lowest position. Matthew 23:12, 19:30; Luke 14:8-11, 18:13-14.*

46. *You must be born again. John 3:3, 5-8.*

47. *Live in me and live in my love. John 8:31-32, 15:4, 9*

48. *Don't covet your brother's blessing. Luke 12:13-15, 15:29-30*

49. *Be baptized. Matthew 29:19, Mark 16:16*

50. *Strive for perfection. Matthew 5:48, John 15:14*[1]

Again, John 14:21 tells us, "He who has My commandments and keeps them, it is he who

---

[1] http://EzineArticles.com/468177 by Matthew Robert Payne. Accessed Oct. 31, 2016.

loves Me. And he who loves Me will be loved by My Father, and I will love him and manifest Myself to him."

Jesus is saying that he has a specific form of love for people who are obedient to him. A few verses later, Jesus says to the disciples in John 15:14, "You are my friends if you do whatever I command you."

Jesus is saying that his disciples are no longer his servants but are now his friends because they do what he commands them to do. As such, we see the importance of the commandments of Jesus.

In the Great Commission at the end of Matthew, Jesus told his disciples to teach everyone everything that he commanded them. In 1 John 2:4, it says, "He who says 'I know him,' and does not keep his commandments, is a liar, and the truth is not in him."

John states this in Revelation 22:15, "But outside are dogs and sorcerers and sexually immoral and murderers and idolaters, and whoever loves and practices a lie."

When John says that the liars are outside the city gates, he is not just talking about people who tell lies. He is talking about people who say that they love Jesus but refuse to obey his commands.

These verses show how important and integral the commandments of Jesus are to a proper Christian life. Obeying these commands is certainly the way to follow God.

Becoming Separate from the World

The scripture that we are going to look at here is 1 John 2:15-17 (New Living Translation)

"Do not love this world nor the things it offers you, for when you love the world, you do not have the love of the Father in you. For the world offers only a craving for physical pleasure, a craving for everything we see, and pride in our achievements and possessions. These are not from the Father, but are from this world. And this world is fading away, along with everything that people crave. But anyone who does what pleases God will live forever."

We must realize that the ways and practices of this world are not what pleases God. We must align our purpose and what we're doing in life with the ways of God.

One of the ways of God is to deny the world and come out of the world.

James 4:4 in the NLT says, "You adulterers![a] Don't you realize that friendship with the world makes you an enemy of God? I say it again: If you want to be a friend of the world, you make yourself an enemy of God."

When we look at that Scripture, we have to realize that the Bible spells out that friendship with the world is adultery.

The Scripture says that if we want to be a friend of the world, then we are an enemy of God. Sometimes I ask people how many of God's enemies he will let into heaven.

The following Scripture in the Bible causes a lot of people worry and concern.

Matthew 7:21-23 states the following: "Not everyone who says to Me, 'Lord, Lord,' shall enter the kingdom of heaven, but he who does the will of My Father in heaven. Many will say to Me in that day, 'Lord, Lord, have we not prophesied in Your name, cast out demons in Your name, and done many wonders in Your name?' And then I will declare to them, 'I never knew you; depart from Me, you who practice lawlessness!' "

I want to focus on two points. Jesus says here that not everyone who says to me Lord, Lord shall enter the kingdom of heaven, but he who does the will of my Father in heaven.

We just read that anyone that does what pleases God will live forever. I am intentionally emphasizing this to make a strong point.

1 John 2:15-17 (NLT) – "Do not love this world nor the things it offers you, for when you love the world, you do not have the love of the Father in you. For the world offers only a craving for physical pleasure, a craving for everything we see, and pride in our achievements and possessions. These are not from the Father, but are from this world. And this world is fading away, along with everything that people crave. But anyone who does what pleases God will live forever."

The verses in Matthew align with the verses in 1 John. The section in Matthew tells us that not everyone who says to me Lord, Lord will enter the kingdom of heaven but everyone who does the will of the Father in heaven. The passage in 1 John tells us not to love the world or anything in the world, and by obeying, you will please the Father in heaven.

You want to be sure that you're doing the will of the Father in heaven.

Jesus says in Matthew 7:23, "And then I declare to them, 'I never knew you, depart from me, you will practice lawlessness.' " We also see that John

15:14 tells us, "You are my friends if you do whatever I command you."

If you're a friend of Jesus, then he won't tell you to depart from him because he knows you. Ponder that thought: you're known by Jesus. In review, to be known by Jesus and to be a friend of his, you need to obey the commands of Jesus. To do the will of the Father in heaven, you need to be divorced from the world.

Again, James tells us that anyone who's a friend of the world is an enemy of God. Again, consider how many of God's enemies he will let into heaven.

How to Divorce the World

We've established that the Lord Jesus had to obey the Word of God. We also need to divorce the world.

James 4:4 calls those who are friends with the world as adulterous, which means they have committed sexual sin with another partner other than God. We need to divorce the world. We need to separate ourselves from the world and from living in it. We need to get rid of the influences of the world in our lives.

How do we do that? One way to live contrary to the world is obey the 50 commands of Jesus. In addition, live God's way and become a friend of Jesus and show your love for him by living for him in the world.

Living the commands of Jesus and the way Jesus taught you to live is a way to live separate from the world. Another way to live separate from the world is by finding out what God wants you to do and aligning your time, your resources and your money with him. Find out what God is doing in the earth and participate in that.

Some people have difficulty spending money on God. They have real trouble tithing to God or giving him their finances. I have found that one of the keys to opening up your ability to give to God is to find a ministry that you are passionate about. Look for a ministry that is impacting the world and making a difference and finance that ministry.

Find a ministry that successfully models loving your neighbor and invest your time and money there. If you have an idea for a ministry that you could start that would really serve your neighbors and demonstrate that you love God, you could start that ministry with your own finances and put your time and resources into that ministry.

Finding Your Purpose in Christ

You can pray and ask God to show you how to live a life pleasing to him so that you can better align your life with his will. The Lord will honor and answer your prayer and show you what to do.

Follow along with this prayer right now.

Dear Father,

I recognize that living your way, living according to the way that you want me to live, is so foreign to me. I realize that I might not be living as you want me to live. Please show me where I can be involved or how I can better serve you.

Please show me the way that you want me to go through clear signs and confirmations. I want to give my life to you. I will start to try and obey your commands. I want to be led in the way that you want me to go. In Jesus' name, Amen.

CHAPTER 3:

Life Founded On The Rock

How to Love with All Your Heart

We have established that one of the things that is important to God is that we love him with all our heart. This begs the question: How do we love God with all our heart?

We have to come to realize what is important to God. We have to spend our time working out individually what matters to God in our life and in the world that we're living.

You might find someone in your church is struggling to financially provide for her family. This might be a single mother who's struggling to support her children on her income.

You might find that God will put it in your heart to help support her. You might find another ministry that's connected with your church that needs more helpers and needs more finances.

You might find that providing them with finances and helping them shows your love for God and service of him in your community.

The world is filled with more needs than there are people to meet those needs. Millions of ministries out there need finances.

How do you love God with all your heart? I've mentioned that before, and I'll mention it again. First of all, you align and live your life according to the commands of Jesus.

Jesus' commands represent the way you love God with your heart and how to love your neighbor. When you love your neighbor, you're loving God. The reverse is also true. When you love God properly, then you will automatically love your neighbor also. When you have the heart of God within you, that love will flow out to your neighbor.

You can love God more completely by knowing and beginning to practice the commands of Jesus.

Of course, you need to ask God for the enabling power of the Holy Spirit so that you can practice the commands of Jesus Christ. You can't just practice the commands of Jesus Christ in your own strength. You need the enabling power of the Holy Spirit to be able to participate in them.

This begs the question: who is your neighbor? Jesus gives us a description in Luke 10:25-37.

And behold, a certain lawyer stood up and tested Him, saying, "Teacher, what shall I do to inherit eternal life?" He said to him, "What is written in the law? What is your reading of it?" So he answered and said, " 'You shall love the Lord your God with all your heart, with all your soul, with all your strength, and with all your mind,' and 'your neighbor as yourself.' " And He said to him, "You have answered rightly; do this and you will live." But he, wanting to justify himself, said to Jesus, "And who is my neighbor?"

Then Jesus answered and said: "A certain man went down from Jerusalem to Jericho, and fell among thieves, who stripped him of his clothing, wounded him, and departed, leaving him half dead. Now by chance a certain priest came down that road. And when he saw him, he passed by on the other side. Likewise a Levite, when he arrived at the place, came and looked, and passed by on the other side. But a certain Samaritan, as he journeyed, came where he was. And when he saw him, he had compassion. So he went to him and bandaged his wounds, pouring on oil and wine; and he set him on his own animal, brought him to an inn, and took care of him. On the next day, when he departed, he took out two denarii, gave them to the innkeeper, and said to him, 'Take care of him; and whatever more you spend, when I come again, I will repay you.' So which of these three do you think was neighbor to him who fell among the thieves?" And he said, "He who showed mercy on him." Then Jesus said to him, "Go and do likewise."

In the story, a priest and a Levite walked past, and they both ignored the wounded man. The Samaritan man came along, and he had compassion on the injured traveler. When traveling through the world, we meet many people in our journey going through difficult times financially, emotionally and spiritually. We have the capacity and the resources to stop and help people. But first, like the Samaritan, we need to have compassion on them.

Who is your neighbor? Your neighbor is anybody. In this story, the Samaritan was a despised race of the Jews. Even so, someone from a different culture, a different race, and someone who was despised took pity on this Jewish person.

In this story, you have to understand that even the lowest Hindu or Buddhist in our world is a neighbor to us. You have to understand that it doesn't matter what the differences are between us and the person that we're helping. We need to help people despite our differences. Sometimes, we even need to help them because of our differences.

As such, we need to find the abilities and the compassion within ourselves to love our neighbor.

How to Love God and Your Neighbor

You might be asking yourself how to love God and love your neighbor.

The simple answer is found in the 50 commands of Jesus. If we live our life according to the 50 commands of Jesus, we will love God and love our neighbor. We have many practical ways and an extensive list of how we can live out our Christian lives.

How do we find balance in life? Some people might think that my life is out of balance. They might say that I spend all my time and resources producing books and materials so that people can learn and grow.

I would say the contrary. I would say that my life, without the ability to produce books, reading materials and resources for people, would be quite empty.

As a prophet, I prophesy to people most days, and as a writer, I spend time editing and recording and involved in what's necessary to produce books.

We need to find balance with our family, our jobs, our vocations and the desire to serve God.

Not everyone has enough free time to spend serving God in everything that they say and do. However, it's important that we find balance between work, family and our life of serving God.

It would help tremendously if you're able to bring God, his presence and his love to your workplace.

God doesn't want us to have a separate Christian life and a separate work life. He wants to be part of your life and demonstrate himself in your life and in your workplace.

You can be godly, righteous and loving in your workplace. Every workplace needs these types of people as influences.

You might wonder how you can do that as you pursue the 50 commands of Jesus. Many of those commands apply to interacting with people. You will spend most of your time and interact the most with others during the week at your job.

You might find that if you start to improve how you interact with others, you'll be able to have an effect on the people that you do life with at your job.

CHAPTER 4:

Finding Your Purpose

If You Won the Lottery, What Would You Do?

If you're not a gambler, which I'm not, just imagine if someone bought you a winning lottery ticket. Imagine if you won $20 million so that you never had to work again for the rest of your life. How would you spend your time? What would you decide to do?

I want you to stop reading for a few minutes and take the time to really ponder that question. Get out a piece of paper and write out a list. Answer these questions. If you had $20 million in your bank account right now, what sort of work would you choose to do? What would you train to do? What type of occupation would you pursue? What lifestyle would you pursue?

When you answer these questions, you will know what you're called to do. Many people have wives or husbands and families, and they're caught up with a job and paying the bills, but they're not doing the job that they were created to do or that they want to do.

Many people are stuck at just doing what they can be paid for, locked into a job that they don't like and that gives them little if any satisfaction.

If you won $20 million, what would you do? Think about that. This is the job that you need to think about pursuing. How can you make adjustments in your life so that you can go after the job that you want?

What Do You Feel You're Meant to Do?

As you thought about the money and the freedom that it would give you, what job did you come up with? What do you feel that you are really meant to do? What do you feel your purpose is? Are you a person who loves people, who's got a lot of time for people and is a really good listener?

Do you feel that you could really do well with training as a spiritual counselor who helps people receive emotional and spiritual healing? Do you have a real interest in educating people? Would you find satisfaction in life by training to become a teacher in a public school or a university? Do you want to pursue a career in ministry, the medical field, the legal field or some type of creative occupation?

What is it that you feel that you are meant to do?

Take some time to invest in your future. It doesn't cost you anything. Take some time and think about what you really want to do.

What makes your heart glad? What excites you? What activities do you organize your life around?

The answer to this is easy for me. I had a past mental illness although I feel that I have been healed at the moment. However, I'm on a disability pension from my government, so I don't have to work. I receive an extra income from giving personal prophecies to people. That income allows me to pay the editor to edit my writing and pay the publisher to publish my books.

I find that I'm able to live quite comfortably on the disability pension so that the earnings from my prophecies can finance the publishing of my books.

As such, financially, life is quite easy and simple for me. I realize that if you're married with children, you have monthly commitments that make it more challenging for you to change jobs. You need an income and might not be able to risk pursuing another occupation. Making a change would be a big decision for you.

You will need to consider all of these factors before you change jobs.

What Does God Say?

Have you heard God's opinion on the matter? Can you talk to God about it? Can you hear him speak to you?

Many Christians only know how to pray one-way prayers. They pray prayers, and God seems to listen, but they can't seem to hear from God themselves. Many people might not be aware of the future or of the job that God wants them to have. This is understandable for many people. You might hesitate to go after a desired vocation if you don't have confirmation from God.

One way to ascertain what God is saying is to have counselors in your life, respected Christians, that you can use as a sounding board.

You can seek counsel from four to five Christians regarding a possible job change. Ask them what they think of the idea and if they think that God would be in it.

You might find that another Christian friend hears from God clearly and would be able to give you direction. However, others have the ability to intuitively feel the presence and the direction of the Holy Spirit.

You might find that God can give you direction if you share your questions with others.

What Do Prophets Say?

Jeremy Lopez, a prophet, provides people with 30-minute life counseling and life direction sessions. During one of those appointments, you can discuss your current job and your desire to work in another field. You can ask Jeremy what God is saying about that and perhaps the steps that you can take to move into that desired job.

If you took the time and paid the fee, which is $200 as of Oct. 26, 2016, for a half-an-hour appointment, it will be well worth your money to find much-needed direction on your life's purpose. After all, money is only money. Our life purpose and direction is a lot more important than money. In addition, if you move into your correct life purpose, you might easily earn that money back with very little time or effort.

While I'm not as skilled as Jeremy Lopez prophetically, I could also seek the leading of the Holy Spirit if you give me a list of occupations that appeal to you. I can provide you with direction and offer you life coaching as well.

Could You Arrange to Do that Job?

You've worked out what you want to do after you've won the $20 million lottery. You've contemplated what job that you really want, and you've asked God or you've asked counselors or people that you respect about it.

Now, you have to work out the details about how you will accomplish it.

You might have asked Jeremy Lopez or me or another prophet about the job. The question that remains is could you arrange to do that job because that is where you need to head. That is the way that you need to go and the direction you need to pursue in life.

It would be such a shame for you to live your life on earth and not do what you're on earth to do.

Not only is life more mundane and lacking purpose when you're not doing what you're destined to do, but it can be really boring. A person might struggle with more addictions, more troubles and negative habits when his or her life is and unfulfilled by what God has purposed for him or her.

I find that my life is a very fulfilled life, a very happy life. The presence of God waxes strong in my life. I'd be really upset if I wasn't doing what God had called me to do.

I'm so fortunate that I've been able to learn what God wants me to do, and he has provided a way for me to do what I am destined to do.

I'm so happy and fulfilled. I'm so loved, and I'm so full of joy with every day that I live. You, too, can reach a stage where you look forward to getting up each morning. You, too, can look forward to achieving your goals in your workplace, and you can look forward to living a more prosperous and happy life that's full of contentment and joy.

CHAPTER 5:

Living Your Purpose

Your Identity in Christ

Many people find their identity in life through the work that they do. While this works well as a way to find fulfillment for some people, it can be disastrous for others.

The best way to measure yourself in the world and in Christ is to find out your identity in Christ.

If you look for books on "your identity in Christ" on Amazon, you'll find many on the subject. I wrote a book by that same name on the topic when I was dealing with my identity in Christ.

The book contains 19 chapters for you as a person who is loved and appreciated by Jesus Christ.

Before we can do any major lasting good in this world, we need to come to love ourselves for who we really are in Christ.

We have to realize that God loves us. We have to realize why God loves us. We have to realize what God loves about us and what God wants to do through us.

We have to realize what our abilities and strengths are and who we really are as Christians in this world. Without knowledge of our identity, without knowledge of what God thinks of us, we might be in an occupation that isn't fulfilling our purpose.

We might feel hopeless, and we might feel that we have a meaningless life and that our life isn't worth much.

Through finding our identity in Christ, we stand on solid ground and live on a firm foundation so that we can go forward with our purpose in life.

First of all, to live out our purpose in life, we need to recognize and understand our identity.

You Are Loved Already

More than anything else — more than the necessity of leaving the world and its cravings behind and more than even knowing and obeying

Jesus' commands — we need to know that before all of that, we are loved by Jesus.

This foundation of the knowledge of his love assures that we're able to pursue the proper Christian life. Jesus wants you to know that you're loved. He wants you to know that he has your whole future planned for you.

He wants you to know that he's the Alpha and the Omega. He's the beginning and the end. He's seen your life. He's seen your struggles. He's seen your future. He's seen everything in your life from start to finish.

Jesus Christ is your Creator, and he knows you. He knows every part of you. He knows you intimately and would love to have a role in your life that sees him directing your life and moving you towards the path that you should take.

He wants to direct you. He wants to lead you. He wants to bring you comfort. He wants to show you his love.

Once you let Jesus love you, once you accept his embrace, once you understand your identity in Christ, you are well on your way to success in this life.

Moving into Your Desired Work

I want to share a personal testimony. Last year, I received a prophecy that God was going to lead me into business and that he was going to give me a business idea.

Between the time that I requested this prophecy and the time that I received it from Jeremy Lopez, I discerned that I could earn extra money by giving personal prophecies to people for donations.

In just the few hours that it took me to send my request to Jeremy and to receive it back, I found a way of earning extra income.

When I received the prophecy from Jeremy, it stated that God was leading me into business to earn an income to better fulfill the desires he had for my life. I soon learned how to start a small business for myself, how to get a business name and how to move forward with the practical aspects of running a business.

Through prophetic words, websites that God led me to and other information, God led me as needed. I am now able to earn from $700 to $1,000 a month by giving prophecies.

I certainly spend that money publishing my books. All of the money that comes from doing personal prophecies is used to publish books. At the moment, I don't really make a profit from my books.

I spend more money producing books than I earn right now, but it's totally fulfilling for me.

So you have to come to a place where you are moving into your desired work.

Jeremy can speak into you to facilitate this process. He releases life-giving words with good direction. However, I have never asked him for a 30-minute session of life direction or life counseling. I do know someone who has used him and who received solid advice from Jeremy. I would suggest that you consider using him or myself to move and transition you into your desired place of work. By doing so, you can find a way of earning an income that better suits your purpose.

Once you've decided what type of work to pursue, you need to make plans on how to transition yourself from your current work to your new work.

You might need to study on a part-time basis to obtain the qualifications to move into your new position. You might have to take time off work and find part-time jobs while you study full time to obtain the new qualifications that you need for your new career path.

Whatever you decide, you will need to make hard decisions and work hard. I know that the enemy of our souls doesn't want to see us living out our purpose and pursuing what we're born to do. The enemy of our souls has a vested interest in keeping us away from our purpose and preventing us from achieving what God wants us to do with our life. The enemy will put up roadblocks and try to stop you from transitioning into your destiny.

However, with solid advice from your friends or from a reputable prophet, you'll be able to sustain those attacks and move on and do what you're destined to do.

Finding Fulfilling Part-Time Occupations

Some people might only need part-time work, depending on their purpose. I have already shared that I don't make a sustainable income from my book sales and that I spend more money producing books than I earn.

So, for me at the present time, publishing books isn't a profitable full-time income yet.

I've shared that I earn a nice income from giving prophecies. However, I spend all of that money producing books, which doesn't produce a profit for me. As such, I spend a lot of my time doing something that brings only eternal rewards but that does not yet sustain me as a full-time occupation.

Similarly, you might have a purpose in this life that will be fulfilled by working part time. You might have a purpose in this life that requires you to spend 10 hours a week doing something that fulfills that purpose. You might find that you are in a full-time job that provides for your wife and your children and financially supports and sustains you. You might not be able to move away from that employment because it is too hard. The transition at this time might be impossible.

You might find instead that God wants you to spend part of your time doing something that achieves your purpose in life. For a season, you might find that your attention to your purpose in life might only be a part-time effort.

Therefore, you might find part-time work that fulfills you. You might find a part-time vocation and allocate your time to it. For me, a part-time allocation of my time is towards the prophecies that I give. This allows people to write to me and request a prophecy so that they are blessed. At the same time, I am earning an income.

You might find some ministries that really serve you well. With your time and effort, you might find this part-time job can fulfill your purpose in life and that you can earn an extra income by doing it.

You might need to research your options. Seek God and find a way that you can work with some of your time doing what God has destined you to do. God might want you to work full-time in one job and work on your purpose and destiny in another job in a part-time capacity.

CHAPTER 6:

Storing Of Rewards In Heaven

What Is a Reward in Heaven?

Matthew 6:19-21 tells us, "Do not lay up for yourselves treasures on earth, where moth and rust destroy and where thieves break in and steal; but lay up for yourselves treasures in heaven, where neither moth nor rust destroys and where thieves do not break in and steal. For where your treasure is, there your heart will be also."

Revelation 22:12 echoes a similar sentiment. "And behold, I am coming quickly, and My reward is with Me, to give to everyone according to his work."

This might not be a popular subject. However, we need to discuss this topic and give it our consideration, especially in this book.

God has destined a great life for you to fulfill. Before each of us come to this earth, God wrote a scroll. And on the scroll, he wrote the plans and the purposes for our lives.

Many people live their entire life without finding those plans or purposes. We've covered some of these subjects about finding that purpose in our life and about living a fulfilling life. We've also talked about being obedient to God.

We need to know about the rewards in heaven for people who do certain things on earth. You can do something as simple as buying a soda for a homeless man and earn rewards in heaven. Rewards in heaven are based on the works that we do on earth.

Scripture clearly says that we are not saved by works, but we are saved by grace. However, we also see in Matthew that Jesus tells us not to store up riches on earth, where moths and rust ruin and thieves break in and steal (Matthew 6:19).

Once again, Jesus is saying that we are not to live in this world with an overabundance of possessions and live in a lifestyle of excess. We are instead to live so that we store up treasure in heaven.

Jesus says in Revelation that he is coming quickly. He is going to bring with him the rewards for the works that we've done. It's clear from those two Scriptures that we can do certain things on earth that will bring eternal rewards.

You don't want to just coast through life, ending up in heaven, just working a normal job and just going to church and listening to sermons all your life and not really achieving much towards loving God and loving your fellow men. If you can, you need to live a life that has a maximum impact on God's Kingdom on earth and the people of earth.

It is important for you to live a life that can impact your fellow man. It's important that you live a life that can change people's lives for the better here on earth.

How Do We Store up Rewards in Heaven?

You can store up rewards in heaven in many ways, such as simply financing your church with your offerings and tithes. Whatever your church achieves, you will share in that reward.

Your church might not have an outreach to the poor or homeless in your city. Instead, they might be better at educating Christians on how to impact others in the city, including the poor and homeless.

Many churches are teaching Christians how to serve God practically, which means that they are laying up treasures in heaven. However, you can just be a Good Samaritan as you walk past a homeless person on the street that has been beaten up by life and dragged down by satan, and you can buy him a drink or something to eat or give him money.

You can give money to charities. You can finance a particular Christian ministry. You can volunteer for Christian ministries. You can find out what really turns you on spiritually and direct your time and resources into that.

God really wants to change the world. He desires to stop injustice in the world. Whatever you do stop injustice will earn you a reward in heaven. God wants people to know him. If people already know him, he wants them to know him better and to obey him.

One way to earn rewards in heaven would be to simply send a book as a gift to some of your friends. You can advertise this e-book on

Facebook and recommend it as an enjoyable read. One way to earn rewards in heaven would be to write a review of this book and say what you honestly think about it.

Whatever you do to further the Kingdom of God on earth will earn you rewards in heaven. In your workplace, whatever you do to show God's love to people will earn you rewards in heaven. Whatever you do with your income that you bring home from work, spending it on your family, loving your family, will earn you rewards in heaven.

The extra income that you send to ministries and that you use to support God's work in the nations will earn you rewards in heaven. Whenever you love God and whenever you love your fellow men, this will earn you rewards in heaven.

As you can see, I am a person who has a lot to say about rewards in heaven. I wrote a book called "Living for Eternity" about living for your purpose and living out your destiny on earth so that you can build up rewards in heaven. It's a bit longer than this book and is rewarding to read.

Personally, I have focused my whole life on rewards in heaven. I only live on this earth to do the absolute will of God, 100 percent, in my life.

My life is only focused on doing everything the Lord commands me to do.

I do everything that the Lord has commanded in the 50 commands of Jesus. I do everything that he directs me to do through his Holy Spirit and through his own voice. The idea for this book came to me as I couldn't sleep at night. God directed me through his Holy Spirit to produce this book that night. He had me record the first draft to this book on audio.

Jesus gave me the title for the book along with the chapter titles and the headings for each of the chapters. I simply followed his directions. In life, it is really handy to learn how to hear from the Holy Spirit and how to take directions from the Holy Spirit and from Jesus. When building your reward in heaven, how exactly do you do that? How do you store up treasure in heaven?

You follow God, and you serve his Kingdom in the best way that you can.

Every person can do more for God. Every person can improve their capacity to serve him. Every person has the ability to change something that they are doing. They can do something better and more efficiently.

I could've chosen to do a number of things tonight when I couldn't sleep — watched TV, surfed the internet, edited another book or many other things to fill in the time. Some of those things were even "good" things. But they weren't what God wanted me to do. Instead, I chose to do what the Holy Spirit directed me to do. I chose to follow his leading and to produce this book. In heaven, I'll receive rewards for writing this book. I will receive credit for everyone who reads this book and who is affected by it. Similarly, you can receive rewards for helping others read this book through advertising it on Facebook or by writing a review on Amazon. Ultimately, people will be affected and will buy this book.

I live for rewards in heaven. You might need to learn more this subject so that you can actively participate in it.

What Does Reward Have to Do with Purpose?

Most importantly, my purpose needs to align with God. When you live your life aligned with God and with his purpose for you, then you live in a perfect place.

Many people haven't found their purpose. I hope through this book that you have found some keys to living in God's purpose. I hope that you have found some of the necessary tools to find that purpose and to walk it out.

If your purpose is loving God and loving your neighbor and if your whole life is aligned accordingly, then you will receive plenty of rewards in heaven. You will be honored in heaven with a place of high importance.

I am not a person who is recognized as someone powerful in the world. But I am a person who spends all of his time participating in and pursuing God's purpose in his life. Even if the world does not view you as important, you can still align your life with the ways of God.

You can make so many changes to your life. You can choose to do so many things to change how you live your life. Do some research on rewards in heaven and on how to build up treasure in heaven. Apply what you learn to your life, and you'll find that your whole life will change and take on a new direction.

As you commit to researching your options, seeking more knowledge and making changes on how you operate your life, you will make a major impact in this world. You can change this world that you live in for the better. You can have a major impact.

Are you going to answer this challenge? Are you going to find your purpose? Are you going to live out your purpose? Are you going to demonstrate the keys to a fulfilling Christian life? Or you are going to continue to live on shifting sands, tossed about by every wind? The decision is up to you. It is **really** up to you.

God bless you.

I'd love to hear from you

One way that you can bless me as a writer is by writing an honest and candid review of my book on Amazon. I always read the reviews of my books, and I would love to hear what you have to say about this one.

Before I buy a book, I read the reviews first. You can make an informed decision about a book when you have read enough honest reviews from readers. One way to help me sell this book and to give me positive feedback is by writing a review for me. It doesn't cost you a thing but helps me and the future readers of this book enormously.

To sow into my book writing ministry, to read my blog or to request your own personal prophecy from God or a life-coaching session, you can visit http://personal-prophecy-today.com. All of your gifts will go toward the books that I write and self-publish.

To write to me about this book or to share any other thoughts that you have, please feel free to contact me at my personal email address at survivors.sanctuary@gmail.com.

You can also friend request me on Facebook at Matthew Robert Payne. Please send me a message if we have no friends in common as a lot of scammers now send me friend requests.

You can also do me a huge favor and share this book on Facebook as a recommended book to read. This will help me and other readers.

How to Sponsor a Book Project

If you have been blessed by this book, you might consider sponsoring a book for me. It normally costs me between fifteen hundred and two thousand dollars or more to produce each book that I write, depending on the length of the book.

If you seek the Holy Spirit about financing a book for me, I know that the Lord would be eternally grateful to you. Consider how much this book has blessed you and then think of hundreds or even thousands of people who would be blessed by a book of mine. As you are probably aware, the vast majority of my books are ninety-nine cents on Kindle, which proves to you that book writing is indeed a ministry for me and not a money- making venture. I would be very happy if you supported me in this.

If you have any questions for me or if you want to know what projects I am currently working on that your money might finance, you can write to me at survivors.sanctuary@gmail.com and ask me for more information. I would be pleased to give you more details about my projects. You can sow any amount to my ministry by simply sending me money via the PayPal link at this address: http://personal-prophecy-today.com/support-my-ministry/ You can be sure that your support, no matter the amount, will be used for the publishing of helpful Christian books for people to read.

Finding Your Purpose in Christ

Other Books by Matthew Robert Payne

The Parables of Jesus Made Simple

The Prophetic Supernatural Experience

Prophetic Evangelism Made Simple

Your Identity in Christ

His Redeeming Love - A Memoir

Writing and Self-Publishing Christian Nonfiction

Coping with Your Pain and Suffering

Living for Eternity

Jesus Speaking Today

Great Cloud of Witnesses Speak

My Radical Encounters with Angels

Finding Intimacy with Jesus Made Simple

My Radical Encounters with Angels - Book Two

A Beginner's Guide to the Prophetic

Michael Jackson Speaks from Heaven

7 Keys to Intimacy with Jesus

Finding Your Purpose in Christ

Conversations with God Book 1

Optimistic Visions of Revelation

Conversations with God Book 2

Coming Soon:

Influencing Your World for Christ: Practical, Everyday Evangelism

You can find my published books on my Amazon author page here: http://tinyurl.com/jq3h893.

About the Author

Matthew was raised in a Baptist church and was led to the Lord at the tender age of 8 years old. Matthew has experienced some pain and darkness in his life, and this has led him to have a deep compassion and love for all people.

Today, he runs two Facebook groups, one called "Open Heavens and Intimacy with Jesus" and one called "Prophetic Training Group." Matthew has a commission from the Lord to train up prophets and to mentor others in the Christian faith. He does this through his groups and by writing relevant books for the Christian faith.

God has commissioned him to write 50 books in his life, and he spends his days writing and earning the money to self-publish. You can support him by donating money at http://personal-prophecy-today.com or by requesting your own personal prophecy or life-coaching session.

It is Matthew's prayer that this book has blessed you, and he hopes it will lead you into a deeper and more intimate relationship with God.

Notes

Notes

Finding Your Purpose in Christ

Notes

Notes

Finding Your Purpose in Christ

www.ingramcontent.com/pod-product-compliance
Lightning Source LLC
Chambersburg PA
CBHW050043080526
44586CB00014B/1430